WESTERN EUROPE TRAVEL GUIDE 2023

Western Europe overview

Western Europe is a district in Europe that ordinarily incorporates nations like France, Germany, Italy, Spain, Portugal, the Unified Realm, Belgium, the Netherlands, Switzerland, Austria, and Luxembourg. The area is portrayed by its created, serious areas of strength for economies government assistance frameworks, exclusive requirements of living, major areas of strength for and authentic ties.

A portion of the significant urban communities in Western Europe incorporate Paris, London, Berlin, Amsterdam, Madrid, and Rome, which are all significant social, political, and financial focuses. The district is home to numerous popular milestones and attractions, for example, the Eiffel Pinnacle, the Colosseum, the Sagrada Familia, and the Huge Ben.

As of late, Western Europe has confronted various difficulties, including political polarization, monetary disparity, migration and outcast emergencies, and the ascent of patriot and egalitarian developments. Be that as it may, the locale stays a significant worldwide power and a significant focus of development, innovation, and culture.

Excellence of Western Europe.

Western Europe is known for its excellence and appeal, with a rich history, stunning scenes, and various societies. Here are probably the most lovely parts of Western Europe:

Memorable urban areas: Western Europe is home to a portion of the world's most noteworthy and beautiful urban areas, like Paris, London, Amsterdam, Barcelona, and Rome. These urban communities are known for their dazzling design, elite historical centers, and rich social legacy.

Normal marvels: Western Europe has a different scene that incorporates the snow-covered Alps, staggering sea shores, moving open country, and old backwoods. A portion of the locale's normal marvels remember the Bluffs of Moher for Ireland, the Norwegian fjords, the Swiss Alps, and the Cinque Terre in Italy.

Craftsmanship and culture: Western Europe has been home to a portion of the world's most renowned specialists and performers, and its historical centers and exhibitions are loaded with extremely valuable show-stoppers. From the Mona Lisa in the Louver to crafted by Van Gogh in Amsterdam, there is no deficiency of imaginative and social fortunes in Western Europe.

Food and wine: Western Europe is known for its heavenly food and wine, with every nation having its own special culinary practices. From French wine and cheddar to Italian pasta and pizza, there is no lack of mouth-watering cooking to attempt.

Celebrations and festivities: Western Europe is home to numerous vivid and energetic celebrations and festivities, like Oktoberfest in Germany, Fair in Venice, and St. Patrick's Day in Ireland. These occasions are an extraordinary method for encountering the locale's way of life and customs.

Generally speaking, the excellence of Western Europe lies in its rich history, shocking scenes, different societies, and novel practices.

Venturing out to Western Europe

Venturing out to Western Europe can be an interesting and remunerating experience. There are various nations and societies to investigate, each with their own one of a kind history, cooking, and attractions.

Before you travel, it's critical to investigate the nations you intend to visit and get to know their traditions, regulations, and social standards. This will assist you with staying away from any errors or social blooper.

As far as useful contemplations, you will require a substantial identification to enter any country in Western Europe, and at times, you may likewise require a visa. Try to check the section prerequisites for every country you intend to visit well ahead of your outing.

With regards to transportation, there are various choices accessible, including trains, transports, and rental vehicles. The rail framework in Western Europe is broad and dependable, going with it a famous decision for some voyagers.

Convenience choices range from spending plan cordial lodgings to lavish inns, and there are a lot of choices to suit all spending plans and inclinations.

A few famous objections in Western Europe incorporate Paris, London, Rome, Barcelona, Amsterdam, Berlin, and Vienna, among others. Every city has its own exceptional person and attractions, so make certain to investigate as needs be to track down the objections that best suit your inclinations.

Generally speaking, heading out to Western Europe can be a superb encounter, however it means a lot to prepare and be ready for the extraordinary difficulties and valuable open doors that accompany investigating another region of the planet.

Normal Food in Europe.

Western Europe includes numerous nations, each with its own remarkable food and conventional dishes. In any case, there are a few normal food varieties that are famous across a few Western European nations. Here are a few models:

Bread: Bread is a staple food in Western Europe, and it is devoured in a wide range of structures. Well known types remember loaves for France, crusty bread in Italy, sourdough in Germany, and soft drink bread in Ireland.

Cheddar: Cheddar is one more staple food in Western Europe, and there are various assortments to browse. Models incorporate cheddar from the UK, brie from France, gouda from the Netherlands, and parmesan from Italy.

Meat dishes: Meat is a well known food in Western Europe, and there are numerous customary meat dishes to attempt. Models remember wieners for Germany, hamburger stews in France, broil meat in the UK, and pork schnitzel in Austria.

Fish: With its long shorelines and admittance to the Atlantic Sea, Western Europe is additionally known for its fish. Models remember fried fish and French fries for the UK, paella in Spain, moules-frites in Belgium, and herring in the Netherlands.

Potatoes: Potatoes are a typical fixing in Western European cooking, and they are much of the time filled in as a side dish. Models remember pureed potatoes for the

UK, french fries in Belgium, and potato gratin in France.

Treats: Western Europe is additionally known for its sweets, with numerous customary desserts and cakes to browse. Models remember apple strudel for Austria, crème brûlée in France, tiramisu in Italy, and waffles in Belgium.

These are only a couple of instances of the normal food sources in Western Europe. There are numerous different dishes and fixings that are famous around here, contingent upon the nation and district.

Western Europe's Way of life.

Western Europe has a rich and different social legacy that incorporates craftsmanship, writing, music, theory, from there, the sky is the limit. A few critical parts of general culture in western Europe include:

Workmanship: Western Europe is home to the absolute most famous craftsmanship historical centers on the planet, remembering the Louver for Paris, the Uffizi Exhibition in Florence, and the Prado in Madrid. The absolute most renowned craftsmen from this area incorporate Leonardo da Vinci, Michelangelo, Vincent van Gogh, and Pablo Picasso.

Writing: Western Europe has a long and rich scholarly practice, with writers like

Shakespeare, Dante, Goethe, and Victor Hugo, among numerous others. Probably the main artistic attempts to emerge from this locale incorporate Wear Quixote, Les Misérables, and Faust.

Music: Western Europe is likewise known for its old style music custom, with writers like Mozart, Beethoven, and Bach hailing from this district. Furthermore, well known music classifications like stone, pop, and electronic dance music have additionally risen up out of Western

Europe, with groups and performers like The Beatles, ABBA, and Dumb Troublemaker.

Reasoning: Western Europe has been a center point of philosophical idea for quite a long time, with persuasive scholars like Plato, Aristotle, and Kant hailing from this locale. Probably the main philosophical developments to emerge from Western Europe incorporate the Edification and Existentialism.

Cooking: Western Europe is known for its different and tasty food, with dishes like pasta and pizza from Italy, croissants and cheddar from France, and wieners and brew from Germany.

These are only a couple of instances of the rich and shifted culture that can be tracked down all through western Europe. Contemplations for Going to Western Europe.

Prior to making an excursion to western Europe, there are a few factors that you ought to consider to assist with guaranteeing that you have a protected and charming outing. Here are a significant things to contemplate:

Visa and Section Necessities: Contingent upon your nation of beginning, you might require a visa to enter western European nations. Ensure you really look at the visa prerequisites and permit sufficient opportunity to get one if fundamental.

Financial plan: Western Europe can be costly, so ensure you plan a sensible financial plan for your excursion. Consider the expense of transportation, convenience, food, exercises, and trinkets.

Climate: The climate in western Europe can fluctuate significantly contingent upon the season and the locale. Check the weather conditions figure before you leave and pack in like manner.

Language: While many individuals in western Europe communicate in English, learning a couple of essential expressions in the nearby language is dependably useful. This can assist you with exploring your strategy for getting around and collaborate with local people.

Transportation: Western Europe has a decent open transportation framework, however it's critical to explore the transportation choices accessible in every country you intend to visit. This will assist you with arranging your agenda and financial plan appropriately.

Wellbeing and Security: While western Europe is for the most part a protected objective, it's as yet vital to play it safe to guard yourself and your possessions. Know about your environmental elements, keep your resources secure, and do whatever it may take to abstain from turning into a casualty of pickpocketing or different sorts of wrongdoing.

Culture: Western Europe is home to a rich and different culture, and it's critical to be conscious of nearby traditions and customs. Research the way of life and customs of the nations you intend to visit, and be aware of your way of behaving and dress out in the open spots.

By taking into account these variables before you leave, you can assist with guaranteeing that your outing to western Europe is a positive and vital experience.

Going to Western Europe

The most straightforward method for going to Western Europe relies upon your beginning stage. The most well-known ways of going to Western Europe are via plane, train, or vehicle.

Plane: Flying is typically the quickest and most helpful method for going to Western Europe, particularly in the event that you're coming from an alternate landmass. Many significant aircrafts offer non-stop trips to significant urban communities like Paris, London, Amsterdam, Madrid, and Rome.

Train: Going via train can be an incredible method for seeing a greater amount of Europe and is in many cases more reasonable than flying. There are a few high velocity rail networks that interface significant urban communities across Western Europe, including the Eurostar among London and Paris, the Thalys among Paris and Amsterdam, and the ICE between Germany, Austria, and Switzerland.

Vehicle: On the off chance that you favor driving, leasing a vehicle can be an incredible method for investigating Western Europe at your own speed. The streets are for the most part very much kept up with, and there are a few panoramic detours to take, for example, the Amalfi Coast in Italy or the German Heartfelt Street.

In general, the least demanding method for going to Western Europe will rely upon your inclinations, spending plan, and schedule. Consider factors like distance, time, cost, and the sort of involvement you need to have prior to settling on the best method of transportation for your outing.

Printed in Great Britain
by Amazon

20966370R00020